BARCELONA

Travel Guide Book

A Comprehensive 5-Day Travel Guide to
Barcelona, Spain & Unforgettable Spanish Travel

• *Travel Guides to Europe Series* •

Passport to European Travel Guides

Eye on Life Publications

Barcelona, Spain Travel Guide Book
Copyright © 2015 Passport to European Travel Guides

ISBN 10: 1518841775
ISBN 13: 978-1518841774

~

All rights reserved. No part of this book may be reproduced in any form or by any electronic or mechanical means, including information storage and retrieval systems, without permission in writing from the publisher, except by a reviewer who may quote brief passages in a review. All photos used courtesy of freeimages.com, HAAP Media Ltd., a subsidiary of Getty Images.

Other Travel Guide Books by Passport to European Travel Guides

Top 10 Travel Guide to Italy

Florence, Italy

Rome, Italy

Venice, Italy

Naples & the Amalfi Coast, Italy

Paris, France

Provence & the French Riviera, France

Top 10 Travel Guide to France

London, England

Amsterdam, Netherlands

Santorini, Greece

Greece & the Greek Islands

Berlin, Germany

Munich, Germany

Istanbul, Turkey

Vienna, Austria

Budapest, Hungary

Prague, Czech Republic

Brussels, Belgium

"It was a spicy night in Barcelona. The air was fragrant and free."—Roman Payne, *The Wanderess*

Table of Contents

Map of Barcelona, Spain..7
Introduction: How to Use This Guide........................9
City Snapshot..10
Before You Go..11
Getting in the Mood
 • What to Read..16
 • What to Watch..17
Local Tourist Information...18
About the Airports...19
How Long is the Flight?..19
Overview of Barcelona..21
★ Insider Tips for Tourists! ★................................23
Spanish Phrases For Emergencies............................28
Climate and Best Times to Travel............................31
Tours
 • By Bike..34
 • By Boat...35
 • By Bus...35
 • By Minibus or Car...36
 • Special Interest or Walking Tours.................36
★ 5 Days in Barcelona ★ Itinerary!
 • Day 1..39
 • Day 2..42
 • Day 3..45
 • Day 4..48
 • Day 5..49
Best Places For Travelers on a Budget
 • Bargain Catalan Sleeps...................................62

- Bargain Catalan Eats..63

Best Places For Ultimate Luxury
- Luxury Catalan Sleeps.......................................55
- Luxury Catalan Eats..57

Barcelona Nightlife
- Great Bars..59
- Great Clubs..60
- Great Live Music..60
- Great Theater...61

Conclusion..63

About the Authors...64

• Map of Barcelona •

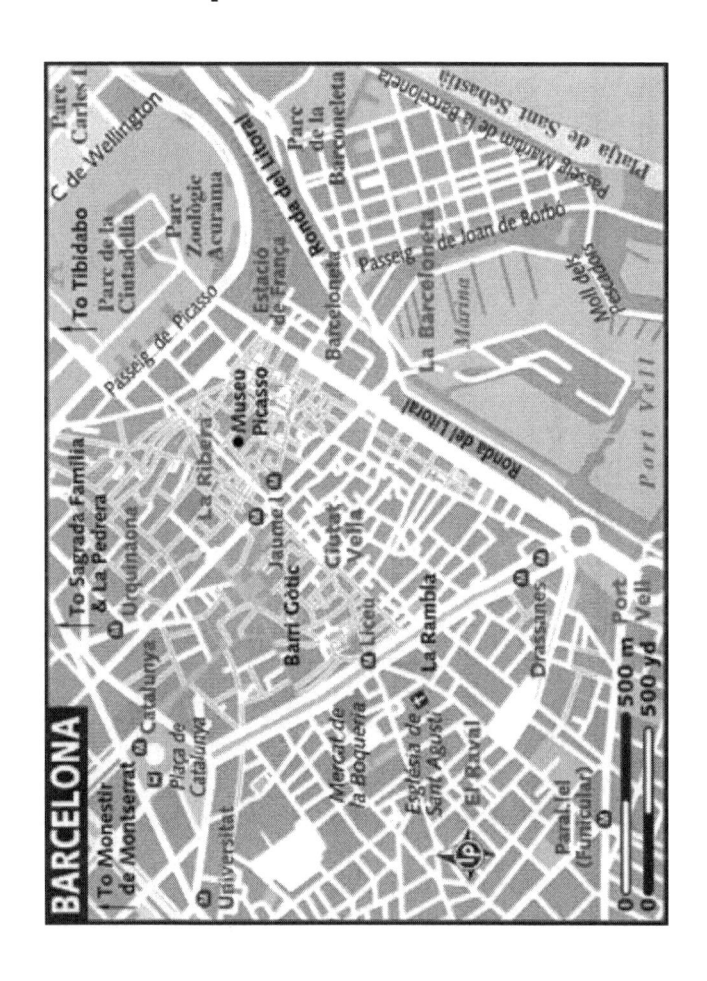

• Introduction •

Barcelona, Spain. Now here's a hip, cosmopolitan city with so much to offer a variety of tastes and personalities. The stunning architecture, the flavorful food and delicious wines, the festive culture, and of course, the relaxing, peaceful lifestyle that puts locals and visitors alike in a fantastic mood!

In this 5-day guide to Barcelona, you'll find a variety of our top recommendations and helpful tips to prepare you for having the best travel experience in Spain's Catalonia region! **Read over the insider tips** carefully and familiarize yourself with the information on preparing for your trip. **Every traveler** has different preferences, and we've included a wide range of recommendations to suit all tastes and budgets.

You're welcome to follow our detailed **5-day itinerary** to the letter, or you can **mix and match** the activities at your own discretion.

Most importantly, we know you're sure to have a great time and enjoy the wonderful city that is Barcelona. Enjoy!

• City Snapshot •

Language: Spanish

Local Airports: Barcelona Airport–El Prat (BCN)

Currency: Euro | € (EUR)

Country Code: 34

Emergencies: Dial 112 (all emergencies) 091 (police) 061 (ambulance) 080 (fire)

• Before You Go... •

✓ Have a Passport

If you don't already have one, you'll need to apply for a passport in your home country a good two months before you intend to travel, to avoid cutting it too close. You'll need to find a local passport agency, complete an application, take fresh photos of yourself, have at least one form of ID and pay an application fee. If you're in a hurry, you can usually expedite the application for a 2-3 week turnaround at an additional cost.

✓ Need a Visa?

U.S. citizens do not require a visa unless they plan to be in Spain (España in Spanish) for more than 90 days. You can use **the following website** to check whether or not you will need to apply for a visa to enter the country: https://spain.visahq.com

✓ Healthcare

For visitors and non-residents, neither emergency nor non-emergency treatment is free. Visitors from outside Europe will have to pay for any medical services and are advised to purchase a traveler's insurance *before* traveling to Spain.

Visitors from within Europe need to carry a valid

EHIC (European Health Insurance Card) and present it at the time of treatment.

Should you have **any minor healthcare issues** (cold, flu, etc.) simply ask someone at your hotel or other accommodation to direct you to the nearest pharmacy (farmàcia).

✓ Set the Date

August is the high season in Barcelona and the busiest month—which means lots of crowds and higher prices. You'll also find that some shops and restaurants close from mid-August to early September, as this is typically when many locals take vacations themselves.

We recommend visiting Barcelona in the off-season **(January to March, October to December).** In the wintertime, temperatures do cool down and can become quite chilly (into the 50s), but it's rarely overbearingly cold.

✓ Pack

- We recommend **packing only the essentials** needed for the season in which you'll be traveling. By far, the most important thing to pack is a good pair of **walking shoes** (water-resistant if you're traveling in colder months, and comfortable, light sandals or sneakers to walk good distances in warmer months).

- Barcelona is a very **fashion-conscious city**, so if you want to blend in, it's a good idea to **dress with style**, especially in the evening.

- If you're planning on visiting any **cathedrals or churches in Barcelona**, be sure to pack **clothes that appropriately cover** your shoulders and legs.

In the colder months, bring a **warm sweater or coat**, and a **rain jacket**. And we always recommend packing **sunscreen, sunglasses, a hat and umbrella.**

- **A backpack** can be handy during the day when you go out sightseeing and collecting souvenirs, particularly when getting on and off buses, boats, trains or trams.

- If you don't speak Spanish, be sure to pack a good **conversational Spanish phrase guide** to bring along with you. You'll find people a lot friendlier toward you if you don't go around assuming they speak your language.

- **Hand sanitizer** is always great to have along with you when traveling.

- **Medication.** Don't forget to have enough for the duration of your trip. It's also helpful to have a **note from your physician** in case you're questioned for carrying a certain quantity.

- A simple **first aid kit** is always a good idea to have in your luggage, just in case.

- You can bring one or two **reusable shopping bags** for bringing souvenirs home.

- **Travelers from outside Europe** will need to bring along a **universal electrical plug converter** that can work for both lower and higher voltages. This way you'll be able to plug in your cell phones, tablets, curling irons, etc., during the trip.

• Be sure to **leave expensive jewels and high-priced electronics at home**. Like most major cities and tourist attractions, thieves and pickpockets abound. Avoid making yourself a target.

• **Take pictures of your travel documents and your passport** and email them to yourself before your trip. This can help in the unfortunate event they are lost or stolen.

• **Pack well,** but be sure to leave room for souvenirs!

✓ Phone Home

How will you call home from Spain? Does your cell phone company offer service while abroad? **What are their rates?**

There are many ways to **call home** from Europe that are inexpensive or completely free.

You may also **sign up for roaming or Internet hotspot** through your own cell phone provider. You can also use Skype, WhatsApp, Viper, or many other voice-over IP providers that are entirely free.

Other options are to buy a **Spanish phone chip** for your phone—which also gives you a local phone number—purchase calling codes before you leave home, or you can buy calling cards or **prepaid cell phones** once you arrive in Spain.

✓ Currency Exchange

Spain uses the **euro** as its currency (same for most of Western and Central Europe). Check out the **currency exchange** rates prior to your trip. You can do so using **the following** or many other online currency exchange calculators, or through your bank. For the best rates, we recommend **waiting until you arrive in Barcelona** to buy euros.

http://www.xe.com/currencyconverter

Also, make sure your bank knows you'll be traveling abroad. This way you avoid having foreign country transactions flagged and declined, which can be extremely inconvenient!

✓ Contact Your Embassy

In the unfortunate event that you should lose your passport or be victimized while away, **your country's embassy** will be able to help you. Be sure to give your itinerary and contact information to a close **friend or family member**, then also contact your embassy with your emergency contact information before you leave.

✓ Your Mail

Ask a neighbor to **check your mailbox** while you're away or visit your local post office and request a hold. **Overflowing mailboxes** are a dead giveaway that no one's home.

• Getting in the Mood •

Here are a few great books and films about, or set in, Barcelona that we recommend you check out in preparation for your trip to this stimulating locale!

What to Read:

Our favorite book set in Barcelona is Carlos Ruiz Zafrón's <u>*The Angel's Game*</u>. A powerful thriller about a struggling pulp fiction writer in Barcelona who's offered a book deal he can't refuse! **This creative tale**, casts the city in an equally romantic and tragic, gothic undertone. It's a great story to delve into before your trip!

In 1936, George Orwell, the great political idealist and writer, went to Spain to report on the Civil War (1936-37) but instead he ended up joining the fight against the Fascists. His famous account, <u>**Homage to Catalonia**</u>, intriguingly describes the war and his experiences in the thick of it. **A true masterpiece**, we think this book really does a great job of brining history to life. You'll see that it was clearly written in great love for the city of Barcelona and the country of Spain as a whole. We think you'll enjoy it!

What to Watch:

If you haven't already seen it, you cannot miss the famous Woody Allen movie, <u>*Vicky Cristina Barcelona*</u>. It's about two American women, Vicky (Rebecca Hall) and Cristina (Scarlett Johansson), spending a summer in Barcelona where they meet an artist, Juan Antonio (Javier Bardem), who is attracted to them both — although still enamored with his mentally and emotionally unstable ex-wife María Elena (Penélope Cruz). **It was shot in Barcelona**, and the Spanish towns of Avilés, and Oviedo. We're sure it'll make you even more excited to travel to Barcelona!

Another really good film set in and about the outskirts of Barcelona, also starring Javier Bardem, is <u>*Biutiful*</u>. Set in the working-class outskirts of the city, the main character Uxbal (Bardem) attempts to raise his two children as a single dad while coping with his mentally imbalanced wife and working with a Chinese immigrants' sweatshop. This one is **rich with emotion and Barcelonian flavor!**

• Local Tourist Information •

Regional tourism authorities have a strong presence on the ground here and can provide lots of useful information. **So once you arrive**, you can seek out their offices for maps, directions, and a healthy dose of supplemental recommendations, which always compliments your travel guides!

Here are the information points we recommend. Be sure to call ahead or visit their websites for the most current hours of operation.

Airport Terminals T1 & T2
Open daily from 8:30 am to 8:30 pm

City Hall at Plaça de Sant Jaume (Main Office)
Address: Plaça de Catalunya, 17, 08002, Barcelona
Phone Number: +34 93 285 3834

Plaça de Catalunya
Address: Plaça de Catalunya, 17-S Barcelona
Phone Number: +34 932 853 834

Estació de Sants (Central Station)
Address: Plaza dels Paisos Catalanes, Barcelona
Phone Number: +34 90 224 0202

Cabina Estació Nord (Central Bus Station)
Address: Estacio Barcelona Nord, Calle d'Ali Bei, 54,

08013, Barcelona
Phone Number: N/A

• About the Airports •

Barcelona Airport-El Prat (BCN) is located approx. 7.5 mi southwest of the center of Barcelona, in the municipalities of El Prat de Llobregat, Viladecans, and Sant Boi. **Airport's website:** http://www.barcelona-airport.com

You can also fly into **Madrid-Barajas airport** and take a smaller airline or train to Barcelona. The high-speed train ride is approximately 3 hours, while the regional train can take 9 hours. **The Madrid airport website is:** http://www.aeropuertomadrid-barajas.com/eng

• How Long is the Flight? •

The Flight to Barcelona:

- **From New York City:** approx. 8 hours

- **From Chicago:** approx. 12 hours

- **From Los Angeles:** approx. 14 hours

- **From Toronto:** approx. 7.5 hours

- **From Moscow:** approx. 4.5 hours

- **From London:** approx. 2 hours

- **From Paris:** approx. 1.5 hours

- **From Hong Kong:** approx. 15.5 hours
- **From Cape Town:** approx. 15.5 hours
- **From Sydney:** approx. 23 hours

The Flight to Madrid:

- **From New York City** is approx. 7.5 hours
- **From Chicago:** approx. 12 hours
- **From Los Angeles:** approx. 11 hours
- **From Toronto:** approx. 7.5 hours
- **From Moscow:** approx. 5.5 hours
- **From London:** approx. 2.5 hours
- **From Paris:** approx. 2 hours
- **From Hong Kong:** approx. 16 hours
- **From Cape Town:** approx. 15.5 hours
- **From Sydney:** approx. 25 hours

• Overview of Barcelona •

Barcelona is located on the beautiful Mediterranean Sea and is the fabulous capital of, and the largest city in, Spain's Catalonia region.

With a dense population of over 1.5 million people, Barcelona is divided into ten official districts, (Barrios as the locals call them), and is known for its diverse, original and **unique architecture,** which showcases the distinctive works of renowned Catalan architect, Antonio Gaudí. **And it doesn't stop there:** the fashionable shopping, the world famous restaurants and signature cuisine, the outdoor markets and fun, the leisurely beach-going lifestyle and more, make the colorful city of Barcelona an increasingly popular European destination year round.

Sightseeing highlights include: Gaudí's as yet unfinished Sagrada Família stylistic church + many of his other phenomenal works, as well as central Barcelona's La Rambla Street, the stimulating Barcelona neighborhoods, any or all of the amazing beaches, and much more!

Not to mention the many hidden, less well-known gems

that await you in this blossoming city...not to worry, we'll be sharing all of Barcelona's secrets with you!

So enjoy the beautifully eclectic city that is Barcelona, Catalonia, Spain—and the rewarding time it has to offer!

• Insider Tips For Tourists •

Etiquette

• **Greeting Etiquette:** It's almost mandatory to shake hands when meeting a stranger, acquaintance or business associate. You may notice locals tend to do lots of hugging, kissing and hand shaking when greeting one another.

• **Dining Etiquette:** Many Spanish restaurants offer designated smoking sections, while others have strict no smoking policies.

If you should be invited to dinner at someone's home, it's appropriate to bring a small gift for the hostess (a bottle of wine, flowers, etc.) and, if they have them, a little something for the children.

• **Smoking Etiquette:** Spaniards are smokers, but the laws in the country are changing these days and smoking is prohibited in all public spaces.

Time Zone

Barcelona is in the UTC (universal time coordinated) + 1 hour time zone. There is a 6-hour time difference between New York City and Barcelona, Spain (Barcelona is ahead on the clock). When it is 8:00 am in New York City, it is 2:00 pm in Barcelona.

The format for abbreviating dates in Europe is different from the US. They use: **day/month/year**. So for example, August 23, 2019 is written in Europe as 23 August 2019, or 23/8/19.

Saving Time & Money

- **Using Spain's public transport system** can help reduce the cost of getting around in Barcelona.

- **We highly recommend** getting the **Barcelona Card!** It gives you **access to the city** in very cost effective and timesaving ways: free use of public transportation, free admission to many tourist attractions, a variety of discounts and even skipping ahead in lines! It's definitely a fantastic value:
http://www.barcelonacard.org

- If you'd like the **premium real estate of beach accommodations** without the hefty hotel rates, go with an **apartment rental!** You'll pay a lot less than if you stayed in a beachfront hotel and you'll have the conveniences of a home:
http://www.tripadvisor.com/VacationRentals-g187497-Reviews-Barcelona_Catalonia-Vacation_Rentals.html

- We also always recommend booking your **flight, hotel accommodations, show tickets,** transportation, etc. as far in advance as possible to avoid higher prices. And if you can help it, avoid traveling during the peak tourism season, between June and August.

- Stroll over to Barcelona's **Boqueria Food Market**

for picnic lunch items and save on eating in restaurants. Anyone can point you to it.

• Visit museums on the days when **admission is free!** Like the Museu Picasso, which is free on the first Sunday of every month; and The Museum of Contemporary Culture, which is free on the first Wednesday of every month.

• **Play ping-pong!** If funds are low, families and friends alike can have fun times in Barcelona at the many free ping-pong tables scattered all over the city.

Tipping

Tipping is common in Barcelona but usually expected from tourists more so than locals. Services charges are generally included in most pricing, but you may want to keep in mind that **salaries in general tend to be low.**

• **Taxi Drivers:** Not expected, but if your driver was especially courteous and didn't take you the long way unnecessarily, you can tip a couple of euros.

• **Hotels:** a tip for helping with your bags, about €1/each bag is greatly appreciated. If you stay more than a few days, you can tip a couple euros to the chambermaid if they do a good job with your room. You're not expected to tip room service.

• **Restaurants:** In general, you can tip a couple extra euros for a meal, however for good service in more upscale restaurants, you should tip 10-15% of the bill.

• **Tour Guides:** If you enjoyed the tour and think the guide did a really good job, you can tip €5-€10 from each person.

When You Have to Go

When you have to go to the bathroom in Barcelona, just ask: **¿Dónde están los servicios?** (Where are the bathrooms?). There shouldn't be a problem finding a restroom in the city: cafés, museums, restaurants, shops, etc.

The restrooms are called **servicios, aseos,** or **lavabos**; "Demas" or "Señoras" for women, and "Caballeros" for men.

Some establishments are for **customers only,** so buying a soda or coffee or other small item is appropriate if you ask to use their restroom.

Be aware that some restrooms you encounter may not have **soap or hand towels** — this is where your **hand sanitizers** will come in handy.

Taxes

Value Added Tax (VAT) a consumption sales tax throughout Europe. As of this writing, the standard rate in Spain is 21%. Reduced VAT rates apply for pharmaceuticals, passenger transport, admission to cultural and entertainment events, hotels, restaurants and on foodstuffs, medical and books.

Visitors from outside Spain may be eligible for a **VAT refund** if certain criteria are met: 1) you do not live in Spain 2) you must retain your receipts and receive a tax free check stamp from customs 3) you must present these to a bank that issues VAT refunds 4) purchases must exceed the minimum of typically €90.15.

Phone Calls

The **country code** for Spain is 34.

When calling home from Barcelona, first dial 00. You will then hear a tone. Then dial the country code (1 for the U.S. and Canada, 44 for the UK, 61 for Australia, 7 for Russia, 81 for Japan, and 86 for China), then the area code without the initial 0, then the actual phone number.

Electricity

Electricity in Spain, as in the rest of Europe, is at an average of **220-230 volts,** alternating at about 50 cycles per second (to compare, the U.S. averages 110 volts, alternating at about 60 cycles per second.) As discussed before, when traveling from outside Europe you will need to **bring an adapter and converter** that enable you to plug your electronics and appliances into **the sockets** they use.

Cell phone, tablet and laptop chargers are typically dual voltage, so you won't need a converter, just an adapter to be able to plug them in. Most small appliances are likely to be dual voltage, but **always double check** when possible, especially to avoid frying hair dryers and travel irons.

In Emergencies

The European emergency number **112** (where calls are answered in English, Italian, French, and German) is not the only emergency number in Spain. You may also use the following emergency numbers in Barcelona: **091** for the police, **061** for an ambulance, and **080** for the fire department.

Spanish Phrases For Emergencies:

No entiendo	I don't understand
Por favor mandeme una Ambulancia.	Please send me an ambulance.
Por favor envie ayuda inmediatamente.	Please send help immediately.
Socorro!	Help!
Por favor, llame a la policía.	Please call the police.
Me siento mal.	I don't feel well.

For any **minor healthcare issues** (cold, flu, etc.) just ask someone at your hotel or other accommodation to direct you to the nearest pharmacy (farmàcia). They're marked with a green cross.

Holidays

Main Public Holidays in Barcelona (banks, government services and most shops and museums close, but most restaurants, cafés and bars stay open):

• January 1 — New Year's Day (Any Nou)
• January 6 — Three Kings Day (Reis Mags)
• April (dates vary) — Good Friday (Divendres Sant), Easter, Easter Monday (Dilluns de Pasqua)
• May 1 — May Day - Labour Day (Festa del Treball)
• June 1 — Fiesta Local (Segona Pascua)
• June 24 — Sant Joan - St. John
• August 15 — Verge de l'Assumpció
• September 11 — National Day Catalunya (Diada de Catalunya)
• September 24 — La Mercè
• October 12 — Spain National Day
• November 1 — All Saints' Day (Tots Sants)
• December 6 — Constitution Day (Día de la Constitución)
• December 8 — La Immaculada

• December 25 — Christmas Day (Nadal)
• December 26 — Boxing Day (Sant Esteve)

Please note that **taxi fares** tend to be higher on public holidays in Barcelona + if the holiday falls on a Thursday or Tuesday, it's common for the Spanish "to make a bridge" ("hacer puente") and take the Friday or Monday off as well to make it a long weekend.

Hours of Operation

Restaurants in Barcelona are usually closed on Sunday nights and on Mondays, and in August some restaurants close for 2-3 weeks when local Barcelonians take vacations.

Banks in Barcelona are open Mondays thru Fridays 8:30 am - 1:00 or 2:00 pm. **ATMs** are available all around the city 24/7

Museums and other tourist attractions in Barcelona are often closed on Monday, but not all. Sites such as La Pedrera, Parc Güell and several other tourist attractions are still open.

Shops typically open 9:00 am - 1/2:00 pm, close for lunch and reopen 4:30 - 8/9/10:00 pm, depending on the shop.

Post offices are usually open Monday thru Friday 9:00 am - 2:00 pm, however the main post office Plaça Antoni López stays open until 9:00 pm and until 2:00 pm on Saturdays.

Money

As we mentioned, Spain's currency is the **euro** (€/ EUR).

It's best not to carry more than **€150-€200 in cash** at any given time. In the event of loss or theft, this will minimize your damages.

It's also best to utilize **ATMs** and tellers in the **non-tourist areas** of the city and be sure to use common sense and not make yourself a target for pickpockets. If anyone approaches you unexpectedly, it's best to politely keep walking.

Also, **beware the unnecessary fees.** If you're given the option to pay in dollars vs. euros when using your credit card, simply say no. Paying in dollars **will cost you more** in fees and you may or may not be informed of the additional charges at the time of the transaction.

• Climate and Best Times to Travel •

As we mentioned, we think visiting Barcelona **January - March or October - December** is best. **Winters do get cold,** but never usually below 50F. Snow is rare, but has happened for a short period of time.

You can expect the **best weather** in Barcelona from **May - July.**

August is hot and very crowded. Temps can climb to the high 90s with humidity that makes it feel even toastier. You can also expect some showers in the summertime.

Transportation

Spain has one of the best **public transportation systems** in all of Europe: a super modern **metro system, buses, well-connected speed rails and tramlines** can shuttle you efficiently all around the city.

The metro system currently has 11 lines: **L1 to L11**. On the street level, stations are marked with a large red 'M' within a diamond.

Licensed taxicabs are black and yellow and abundant throughout the city. **A green light** on the roof indicates the cab is available.

Driving

With the terrific public transportation system, we do not recommend visitors drive in Barcelona. This city has one of the **highest accident rates** in Europe. And if that isn't enough, **parking** can be quite expensive and cars are promptly **towed** away if left in even remotely questionable spots.

However, should you still decide to **rent a car** and drive while in Barcelona, they drive on the right-hand side of the road and overtake on the left; you must be at least 18; have your current driver's license, passport and valid insurance; a set of bulbs and spare tire with tools for replacing if necessary; and two red warning triangles approved by the Ministerio de Interior (Internal Ministry).

• Tours •

By Bike

Fat Tire Bike Tours offers a variety of awesome cycle tours around the city of Barcelona and they're our personal favorite. You can spend a half-day (or all day) experiencing the city via bike ride. Tours are led in English and are quite enjoyable!

Fat Tire Bike Tours
Address: Carrer de Sant Honorat, 7, 08002, Barcelona
Phone Number: +34 933 429 275
http://barcelona.fattirebiketours.com/barcelona/tours

The Viator offers a **4-hour cycling tour** that we really like. You get an introduction to Barcelona's rich history in addition to many of the main attractions along the way, including the Placa Sant Jaume, Placa del Rei, La Sagrada Familia, Port Vell, etc. You can book easily online or call.

Viator
Phone Number: +888-651-9785
http://www.viator.com/tours/Barcelona/Barcelona-Half-Day-Bike-Tour/d562-3993FTBB

By Boat

We totally love this **3-hour Mediterranean sailing trip** of some of the best attractions in Barcelona! It's perfect for a relaxing evening on the waterways. It's the best and we know you're bound to love this!

Viator
Phone Number: +888-651-9785
http://www.viator.com/tours/Barcelona/Private-Tour-Barcelona-Sailing-Trip/d562-5571PARTYSAIL

By Bus

The British company, **Worldwide City Sightseeing Hop-On Hop-Off,** offers a really nice bus tour that runs two different routes with a third during the high season, April thru October. All routes have 44+ stops around Barcelona and offer their own perspectives for experiencing the city.

Barcelona City Sightseeing Hop-On Hop-Off Tour
Phone Number: +34 932 853 832
http://www.city-sightseeing.com/tours/spain/barcelona.htm

By Minibus or Car

Another great Viator offering is a fantastic group day trip to **Montserrat and Cava Trail!** It is a small group tour rich in Spanish history, short hikes into the mountains, wine tastings, and delicious food. The drive to Montserrat is about 1.5 hours. You ride in a comfortable minivan with a professional, English-speaking guide. Very nice.

Viator
Phone Number: +888-651-9785
http://www.viator.com/tours/Barcelona/Montserrat-and-Cava-Trail-Small-Group-Day-Trip-from-Barcelona/d562-3142MONT

Try Special Interest or Walking Tours

Are you on vacation in Barcelona with the kids and family? **Runner Bean Tours** has a super fun **Kids & Family Walking Tour** that's sure to delight little ones and grown-ups alike with a variety of magical excitement that's uniquely Barcelona!

Runner Bean Tours Barcelona
Address: Carrer del Carme 44, pral 2ª 08001, Barcelona
Phone Number: +34 636 108 776
http://www.runnerbeantours.com/barcelona-tours/walking-tour-kids-y-family/7

We also think the **Viator's Hot Air Balloon Tour Over Catalonia** is not to be missed! You set out early in the morning and it goes for about 2 hours where you're rewarded with scrumptious views of the Pyrenees, Montserrat, and of course the gorgeous Mediterranean Sea. There's a nice brunch after the tour.

Viator
Phone Number: +888-651-9785
http://www.viator.com/tours/Barcelona/Hot-Air-Balloon-Flight-over-Catalonia/d562-2646BCNBALLOON

Have you read and enjoyed **Carlos Ruiz Zafón** celebrated bestseller, **The Shadow of the Wind?** Then you must check out **The Shadow of the Wind Walking Tour!** A tour guide escorts you and covers key locations from the story — off the tourist grind and into the real Barcelona. Fans of the book won't want to miss it!

Viator
Phone Number: +888-651-9785
http://www.partner.viator.com/en/15868/tours/Barcelona/The-Shadow-of-the-Wind-Walking-Book-Tour-in-Barcelona/d562-5574BCNMOVIESHADOW

Ever been curious about Christopher Columbus? We think you'll enjoy this **3.5-hour walking tour by Mythical Cultural Management Company!** It reveals some little-known mysterious facts about the legendary sea voyager!

Discovering Columbus
Phone Number: +34 932 853 832
http://www.mitic.cat/php/ls.php?fx=t73_eng&fz=

dcr

There's also a wonderful tour of **Jewish Barcelona** by a great company called, **Hi. This is Barcelona...** For about 2.5 hours, an expert guide will introduce you to Barcelona's substantive Jewish history and points of interest.

Hi. This is Barcelona...
Address: 08013, Barcelona, Spain
Phone Number: +34 625 868 612
http://www.hithisisbarcelona.com/tour-jewish-barcelona

And finally, why not see Barcelona from the friendly skies? **Viator's Barcelona City and Coast Helicopter Tour** is a dynamite experience! In about 12 minutes, you'll fly over the most iconic sites in the city! Such fun!

Viator
Phone Number: +888-651-9785
http://www.viator.com/tours/Barcelona/Barcelona-City-and-Coast-Helicopter-Tour/d562-5567BCNCITYHELI

• 5 Days In Barcelona! •

Enjoy this 5-day itinerary for a well-balanced and fun-filled experience in Barcelona! Modify or adjust if you like! Also, be sure to **check websites or call ahead** for the most recent hours and pricing information. Enjoy!

• Day 1 •

Barcelona is a big city but very walkable in a 5-day period. You can also **rent a bike** to get around town.

Once you arrive at your hotel (or wherever you're staying) relax a bit, get settled and then freshen up before venturing out to begin your Catalonia adventure. (It's best to arrive in the morning.)

Why not begin your time in Barcelona with one of this city's staple tourist attractions? Head over to the gorgeous **Basílica de la Sagrada Família**, a monumental Roman Catholic church designed in 1882 by renowned Catalan architect, **Antoni Gaudí**, in a stylized combination of Gothic and Art Nouveau touches.

Even if you don't go inside (there's often a long line!) we definitely recommend seeing this church from the outside. Construction began in 1882 and is *still* ongoing due to years of financial delays, civil wars and the like. Incredible, right?

After that, if you're hungry, grab a bite at the nearby **La Taqueria** Mexican restaurant! Due to the location, the prices are admittedly tourist-driven, but they serve some of the best tasting tacos in Barcelona!

And after lunch, there's much more **Antoni Gaudí** to see around the city. Even if you know nothing about architecture or Gaudí's work, you'll be able to identify his work anywhere after seeing Basílica de la Sagrada Família.

Next we recommend checking out his first principal work, **Casa Vicens**, an amazing private residence built for a wealthy local family in 1888. Located in Barcelona's Grácia neighborhood, we think it's highly underrated.

La Pedrera (Casa Milá), Gaudí's final civil work is a must see! It's more sculpture than building.

You're probably fatigued after a long day of traveling and seeing today's initial sights, so we recommend having **dinner at your hotel** or at a nearby restaurant before turning in for a great night's rest. Tomorrow awaits!

Location Information

Basillica de la Sagrada Família
Address: Carrer de Mallorca, 401, 08013, Barcelona
Phone Number: +34 935 132 060

http://www.sagradafamilia.org/en

La Taqueria (Restaurant)
Address: Passatge de Font, 5, 08013, Barcelona
Phone Number: +34 931 261 359
http://www.lataqueria.eu

Casa Vicens
Address: Carrer de les Carolines, 18-24, 08012, Barcelona
http://www.casavicens.es

La Pedrera
Address: Provença, 261-265, 08008, Barcelona
Phone Number: +34 902 202 138
https://www.lapedrera.com/en/home

• Day 2 •

After a nice breakfast at your hotel, set out for **Parc Güell**, one of Barcelona's most iconic and recognizable attractions! **Antoni Gaudí** built this geometric park between 1900 and 1914, and today it's part of the UNESCO World Heritage Sites. It is a unique garden complex on Carmel Hill that houses a series of interesting architectural structures, including Gaudí's own home, now the **Gaudí House Museum**: http://www.casamuseugaudi.org/cm-eng

For lunch, we recommend the nearby **Maigot Café**. Delicious salads, pizzas and sandwiches here, and the people are super friendly!

From there, head over to **Palau Güell**, another masterpiece designed by Gaudí as a private residence for industrial tycoon, Eusebi Güell. It was used as a backdrop in the Jack Nicholson-Maria Schneider film, *The Passenger* from 1975.

Another must see tourist attraction in Barcelona is **Camp Nou** — the famed soccer stadium of the world famous Futbol Club Barcelona (Barça)! Camp Nou is Europe's largest football stadium and the 2nd largest capacity football stadium in the world!

And if you're a football fan (or traveling with one), you must tour the **FCB Musuem** at Camp Nou. The feature highlight is the view of the stadium from the gallery — it's spectacular!

If you have time this evening, visit **La Boqueria** market (Mercat de Sant Josep de la Boqueria), the largest, oldest, and finest marketplace in Barcelona! The covered areas date back to 1840, but the open-air spots date to the Middle Ages, when they started selling meat there! You can shop for **souvenirs**, **clothing** and of course, the some of the best **produce** Spain has to offer!

You can find a **picnic style dinner** here if it suits you, or head over to **El Quim de la Boqueria!** Right in La Boqueria, El Quim serves up delicious seafood and tapas, the must have staple in Spanish cuisine!

Location Information

Parc Güell
Address: Carrer d'Olot, s/n, 08024, Barcelona
Phone Number: +34 902 200 302
http://www.parkguell.cat/en

Palau Güell
Address: Carrer Nou de la Rambla, 3-5, 08001, Barcelona
Phone Number: +34 934 725 775
http://palauguell.cat/en

Maigot Café
Address: Carrer de la Mare de Déu del Coll, 71, 08023, Barcelona
Phone Number: +34 932 101 223

Camp Nou & FCB Museum
Address: Avinguda Aristides Maillol, 12, 08028, Barcelona
Phone Number: +34 902 189 900
Main Website: http://www.fcbarcelona.com/camp-nou

FCB Museum Website:
http://www.fcbarcelona.com/camp-nou/detail/card/fcb-museum

La Boqueria
Address: Plaza de la Boqueria | Ramblas, 08001, Barcelona
Phone Number: +34 933 18 25 84
http://www.boqueria.info/index.php?lang=en

El Quim de la Boqueria
Address: Mercado de La Boqueria, Les Rambles, 91, 08002, Barcelona
Phone Number: +34 933 019 810
http://elquimdelaboqueria.cat

• Day 3 •

How about a jaunt to the beach today? (Beach is "**playa**" in Spanish, "**platja**" in Catalan) Hop a short train ride over to **Nova Icária Beach** for a great day of fun in the sun! We love this beach most because it's peaceful and has lots of amenities, such as free Wi-Fi, showers, table tennis, volleyball, disabled beach-goer assistance, children's area, and more! There are also plenty of good nearby options for lunch and dinner, or you can bring along a picnic basket from your time in the market.

From here, you'll also be close to the Icária shopping center where there's a VO (Version Originale), original language movie theater showing films in their original language. So lots of English language films. So after a great day on the beach, you can catch a movie at **Yelmo Icària Cinema.**

While there are several beaches in Barcelona, **Barceloneta Beach** being the most popular, there are lots of crowds there and, in our experience, it's not as clean as others. Not one of our favorites, we would avoid it.

Barcelona also has a nude beach if you're interested. **La Mar Bella Beach** is the only official nudist beach in Barcelona. (Address: Passeig de Garcia Faria, 08019, Barcelona, Spain)

Alternatively, if you're not a beach-lover, today's perfect for one of **our recommended tours**. Why not call ahead and book Viator's private **3-hour Mediterranean boat tour**, and Runner Bean's **Kids & Family Walking Tour** for today?

For dinner tonight, we recommend **Petit Pau Restaurant**, one of the best in the city. We think they have some of the best steaks and seafood in all of Spain!

Location Information

Platja de la Nova Icária (Beach)
Address: Passeig Marítim de Nova Icària, 08005, Barcelona
Phone Number: +34 932 85 38 34

Yelmo Icària Cinema
Address: Calle Salvador Espiriu, 61, El Centre de la Vila, Port Olimpic, 08005, Barcelona
Phone Number: +34 932 217 585
http://www.yelmocines.es/cine/yelmo-cines-icaria

Viator (Mediterranean Boat Tour)
Phone Number: +888-651-9785
http://www.viator.com/tours/Barcelona/Private-Tour-Barcelona-Sailing-Trip/d562-5571PARTYSAIL

Runner Bean Tours Barcelona
Address: Carrer del Carme 44, pral 2ª 08001, Barcelona
Phone Number: +34 636 108 776
http://www.runnerbeantours.com/barcelona-tours/walking-tour-kids-y-family/7

Petit Pau Restaurant
Address: Carrer de l'Espanya Industrial, 22, 08014, Barcelona
Phone Number: +34 933 313 275

https://www.facebook.com/pages/Petit-Pau-Restaurant/234136820076860

• Day 4 •

It's day trip time! Time to leave Barcelona (briefly) to see the famous **Montserrat Mountains**. Go ahead and book the **Montserrat and Cava Trail** Viator tour, it's a great value and a memorable experience, with short hikes, good food and wine tastings. Enjoy day four!

Viator
Phone Number: +888-651-9785
http://www.viator.com/tours/Barcelona/Montserrat-and-Cava-Trail-Small-Group-Day-Trip-from-Barcelona/d562-3142MONT

• Day 5 •

Today can be easygoing and relaxed with unstructured time since you're just back from a day trip, or you can get out and about with the full day of new adventures we've outlined for you below!

After a nice, unhurried breakfast at your hotel, don't miss **Las Ramblas**, Barcelona's most popular and busy, tree-lined street (or streets rather, there are five of them). Everything's happening here, it's an **open pedestrian mall** with a local twist. Cobblestoned and lined with gorgeous trees, it's a great place to spend your fifth day, strolling through in the morning, before the afternoon crowds set in. If you're looking for great shopping, Las Ramblas is the place to be!

And don't miss the **statue of Christopher Columbus** on the southern end of the main street. You can also see **Port Vell** from here, a waterfront harbor and old port of Barcelona.

One word of caution about the Las Rambla area: beware of pickpockets. Hold your purse and bags securely, and it's best not to walk around with your phone, wallet or any other valuable in your back pocket.

For lunch, head over to **Elisabets.** We think it's a cool atmosphere and just enough out of the "tourist trap" domain to be a great spot for local fare like tapas, Mediterranean sandwiches and more.

East of Las Ramblas is **Barcelona's Gothic Quarter** (Barri Gotic) The labyrinthine street design makes this walkable area a must see—and provides many **Ko-**

dak moments!

Next, you can make your way to see the **Museu Picasso** (The Picasso Museum) where you'll find one of the most comprehensive and extensive collections of **Pablo Picasso's** artworks. Picasso's wonderful relationship with Barcelona is beautifully demonstrated and preserved here.

For dinner this evening, don't miss the nearby **Taperia Princesa**! Fast, delicious Spanish and Mediterranean fare in a nice atmosphere. Have a nice sangria and enjoy!

And if you're looking for something to do this evening, you can always check out an **outdoor movie screening**. The weather's usually perfect for watching movies outdoors, and Barcelona's hosting more and more film festivals over the last few years. Among the screenings spots is the **Sala Montjuïc**, which offers classic films, concerts and even tours of the Montjuïc Castle! Check their website ahead of time for show times and tickets.

Location Information

Las Ramblas (Shopping District)
Address: La Rambla, Ciutat Vella, 08002, Barcelona
http://www.barcelonaturisme.com/wv3/en/page/160/la-rambla.html

Elisabets (Restaurant)
Address: Carrer d'Elisabets, 2-4, 08001, Barcelona
Phone Number: +34 933 175 826

http://www.tripadvisor.com/Restaurant_Review-g187497-d693967-Reviews-Elisabets-Barcelona_Catalonia.html

Gothic Quarter, Barcelona
Address: Mediterranean Seafront to Ronda de Sant Pere, Ciutat Vella, 08002, Barcelona
http://www.tripadvisor.com/Attraction_Review-g187497-d190162-Reviews-Gothic_Quarter_Barri_Gotic-Barcelona_Catalonia.html

Museo Picasso
Address: Carrer de Montcada, 15-23, 08003, Barcelona
Phone Number: +34 932 563 000
http://www.museupicasso.bcn.cat/en

Taperia Princesa
Address: Carrer de la Princesa, 20, 08003, Barcelona
Phone Number: +34 632 272 392
http://www.tripadvisor.com/Restaurant_Review-g187497-d2547681-Reviews-Taperia_Princesa-Barcelona_Catalonia.html

Sala Montjuïc (Open-Air Cinema)
Address: Carretera de Montjuic, 66, Barcelona
Phone Number: +34 933 023 553
http://salamontjuic.org/en

• Best Places For Travelers on a Budget •

In Barcelona, finding (decent) accommodations under €100 per night can be a challenge, but not to worry — we've got three fabulous recommendations for you if you're on a budget, just take your pick!

Bargain Catalan Sleeps

Our favorite budget option is Hotel España. Around the corner from La Rambla, it's in a fabulous location with a wonderfully transporting atmosphere — you might feel as if you're in the days of famed Catalan architect, Antoni Gaudí himself!

Hotel España
Address: Carrer Sant Pau, 9-11, 08001, Barcelona
Phone Number: +34 935 500 000
http://www.hotelespanya.com/en

Hostal Grau Barcelona is another awesome option just one block from La Rambla, and particularly good for the **environment-friendly** traveler! This charming and "echo-chic" boutique hotel boasts a "go green" philosophy and promises to enchant guests with more than just friendly room rates.

Hostal Grau Barcelona
Address: Carrer de les Ramelleres, 27, 08001, Barcelona
Phone Number: +34 933 018 135
http://www.hostalgrau.com/en/hotel-overview.html

Centrally located in the city center, Barcelona's **Hostal Goya** is one of the better budget options you can find. They have nineteen nicely decorated and historically fashioned rooms. You can also get private apartments with small kitchens that can accommodate groups of up to 6 people.

Hostal Goya
Address: Calle Pau Claris, 74, 08010, Barcelona
Phone Number: +34 933 022 565
http://www.hostalgoya.com

Bargain Catalan Eats

The Mexican restaurant, **La Taqueria**, is budget-friendly despite being just around the corner from La Sagrada Familia Roman Catholic Church, and is a choice lunch spot. The tacos and nachos and tacos are delicious here.

La Taqueria (near La Sagrada Familia)

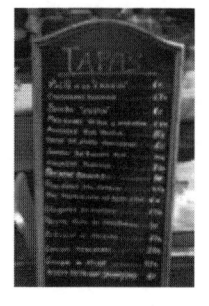

Address: Passatge de Font, 5, 08013, Barcelona
Phone Number: +34 931 261 359
http://www.lataqueria.eu

Mosquito is a great tapas restaurant with equally good beers and fantastically good Chinese dumplings! Located in the heart of Barcelona's Born district, Mosquito serves up really tasty Asian/Vietnamese/Chinese fare, some of our favorites!

Mosquito
Address: 46 Carrer dels Carders, 08003, Barcelona
Phone Number: +34 932 687 569
http://www.mosquitotapas.com/mosquito/en

Elisabets is a great, old-fashioned restaurant with huge portions and plenty of local regulars. They serve yummy tapas, sandwiches, and other traditional Catalonian cuisine.

Elisabets
Address: Carrer d'Elisabets, 2-4, 08001, Barcelona
Phone Number: +34 933 175 826
http://www.tripadvisor.com/Restaurant_Review-g187497-d693967-Reviews-Elisabets-Barcelona_Catalonia.html

• Best Places For Ultimate Luxury •

Luxury Catalan Sleeps

Our number one hotel recommendation for ultimate luxury in Barcelona has to be **Mercer Hoteles Barcelona!** Classy, elegant ambiance, eager to please staff, and rooms that offer the best in high-end accommodations with some of the most comfortable beds in town! You can't go wrong with this gem of a hotel.

The Mercer is tucked away on an "off the way" street and some cab drivers may have a hard time finding it, so it's helpful to **print out the directions** from the hotel's website to give to your driver:
http://www.mercerbarcelona.com/en/location-directions

Mercer Hoteles Barcelona
Address: Carrer dels Lledó, 7, 08003, Barcelona
Phone Number: +34 933 107 480
http://www.mercerbarcelona.com/en

El Palace Hotel Barcelona is another fabulous luxury hotel we love booking. Centrally located (near the Gothic Quarter, Las Ramblas, and attractions like the Picasso Museum and La Sagrada Famillia), El Palace is also distinguished by the fact that famed Spanish artist, Salvadore Dalí, and his wife, Gala, had lived in its Royal Suite, now his name sake: the **Salvadore Dalí Suite**.

Hotel El Palace Barcelona
Address: Gran Via de les Corts Catalanes, 668, 08010, Barcelona
Phone Number: +34 935 101 130
http://hotelpalacebarcelona.com/en

Another marvelous and beautiful high-end accommodation is the **Majestic Hotel & Spa!** How dynamite is this location? It's in the heart of Barcelona! On the Passeig de Grácia, one of Barcelona's chief shopping areas; it's a mere ten-minute walk from Les Rambles; there's an abundance of shops, restaurants, and even a supermarket nearby — Majestic is perfection all around!

Majestic Hotel & Spa Barcelona
Address: Passeig de Gràcia, 68-70, 08007, Barcelona
Phone Number: +34 934 881 717
http://www.hotelmajestic.es/en

Luxury Catalan Eats

One of our favorite spots for the epitome of fine dining in Barcelona is **Cinc Sentits**. They serve delicious and wonderfully presented Catalan cuisine in a superb ambiance. Makes for a great night!

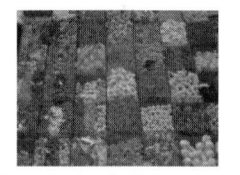

Cinc Sentits
Address: Carrer d'Aribau, 58, 08011, Barcelona
Phone Number: +34 933 239 490
http://cincsentits.com/en

Not only is the high-end Catalan fare at **Restaurant Casa Calvet** delectable, but you literally dine inside a breathtaking piece of art by Antoni Gaudí himself! We're hard pressed to find a more apropos Barcelona dining experience. Be sure to call ahead for reservations. They book up fast and are closed on Sundays.

Casa Calvet Restaurant
Address: Carrer de Casp, 48, 08008, Barcelona
Phone Number: +34 934 124 012
http://www.casacalvet.es/index.php?lang=en

ABaC Restaurant is one of the best modern Catalan restaurants in Barcelona. They provide everything you want in luxury dining: an intimate and romantic ambiance; beautiful, sophisticated décor; and of course scrumptious cuisine, fine wines, and delectable desserts!

ABAC
Address: Avenida del Tibidabo, 1, 08022, Barcelona

Phone Number: +34 933 196 600
http://www.abacbarcelona.com/en/restaurant

• Barcelona Nightlife •

Great Bars in Barcelona

Bar Calders is our favorite bar in Barcelona. Named after the Catalan writer Pere Calders, you can peruse some of his works and even buy a book while sipping your martini! Bar Calders has a great selection of tapas, and a wide variety of alcoholic beverages.

Bar Calders
Address: Calle Parlament 25, 08015, Barcelona
Phone Number: +34 933 299 349
https://ca-es.facebook.com/pages/Bar-Calders/139640212768112

Absenta is an intimate bar setting where you can enjoy good drinks, tapas and light snacks. It's a dark night ambiance with an 'old-fashioned bar' feel. An enjoyable time if this is your type of setting!

Absenta Bar
Address: Carrer de Sant Carles, 36, 08003, Barcelona
Phone Number: +34 932 213 638
http://www.absentabar.es/indexe.html

Great Clubs in Barcelona

Macarena Club is an underground gem in Barcelona. It's a little rough around the edges but very popular, especially with locals. They play underground house, techno and non-commercial dance music for big crowds each night. Lots of fun here!

Macarena Club
Address: Carrer Nou de Sant Francesc, 5, 08002, Barcelona
Phone Number: +34 933 013 064
http://macarenaclub.com

Moog is a tiny, two-floor club with a well-deserved rock star reputation on the Barcelona nightlife scene. It's in the heart of downtown Barcelona and is devoted to electronic/techno music, but even if they're not your cup of tea, we still recommend dropping by Moog! The vibe is pure exhilarating fun and there's even a non-smoking dance floor!

Moog Club
Address: Carrer de l'Arc del Teatre, 3, 08002, Barcelona
Phone Number: +34 933 191 789
http://www.masimas.com/en/moog

Great Live Music in Barcelona

Sala Razzmatazz is a large venue for great live music entertainment: electro rock, electro pop, techno pop, and indie rock. Genre bands from all over the world perform here! Check the website for upcoming bookings!

Sala Razzmatazz
Address: Carrer Almogàvers, 122, 08018, Barcelona
Phone Number: +34 933 208 200
http://www.salarazzmatazz.com

Sidecar Factory Club is another of the city's great live music venues. Sidecar will feed your indie rock passion like no other spot in Barcelona. It's a super popular club, so make sure to book your tickets way in advance!

Sidecar Factory Club
Address: Plaça Reial, 7, 08002, Barcelona
Phone Number: +34 933 021 586
http://www.sidecarfactoryclub.com

Great Theatre in Barcelona

Teatre Nacional de Catalunya (The Catalan National Theatre) features mostly Catalan productions, but you can catch the occasional international production here as well. If you love the theater, you definitely want to book a show here.

The Catalan National Theatre
Address: Plaça de les Arts, 1, 08013, Barcelona
Phone Number: +34 933 065 700
http://www.tnc.cat/en

Gran Teatre del Liceu is the second largest opera house in Europe and we love taking in a show here! It's perfectly situated on the La Rambla, Barcelona's main street. You can also tour this amazing 18th century building daily with a variety of pre-arranged tours you can book online.

Gran Teatre del Liceu
Address: La Rambla, 51-59, 08002, Barcelona
Phone Number: +34 934 859 900
http://www.liceubarcelona.cat/en.html

• Conclusion •

Barcelona is by far one of the most interesting, happening cities in Spain, if not the whole of Europe! It rivals Milan and Madrid on the leader board of Spain's top destinations.

So we hope you have found our guide to the colorful, Catalan city of Barcelona helpful and wish you a safe, interesting, and fun-filled trip to Spain!

Warmest regards,

The Passport to European Travel Guides Team

Visit our Blog! Grab more of our signature guides for all your travel needs!

http://www.passporttoeuropeantravelguides.blogspot.com

★ **Join our mailing list** ★ to follow our Travel Guide Series. You'll be automatically entered for a chance to win a **$100 Visa Gift Card** in our monthly drawings! Be sure to respond to the confirmation e-mail to complete the subscription.

• About the Authors •

Passport to European Travel Guides is an eclectic team of international jet setters who know exactly what travelers and tourists want in a cut-to-the-chase, comprehensive travel guide that suits a wide range of budgets.

Our growing collection of distinguished European travel guides are guaranteed to give first-hand insight to each locale, complete with day-to-day, guided itineraries you won't want to miss!

We want our brand to be your official Passport to European Travel — one you can always count on!

Bon Voyage!

The Passport to European Travel Guides Team
http://www.passporttoeuropeantravelguides.blogspot.com